TYRANNY

AT

THE WATERS' EDGE:

"DRAINING THE

SWAMP!"

by

Dennis Andrew Ball, author

THE BALL DOCTRINE:

"Creating Peace & Prosperity In Every Nation!"

Copyright © 2018 Dennis Andrew Ball

All rights reserved.

ISBN 13: 978-1725825451
10: 1725825457

<u>DEDICATION</u>

"THIS BOOK IS DEDICATED TO AMERICANS WHO SACRIFICE EVERYDAY TO PRESERVE PROTECT & DEFEND OUR LIBERTY & FREEDOM FOR OUR CHILDREN& GENERATIONS TO COME!

NOW THE TIME HAS COME FOR A NEW GENERATION OF AMERICANS TO TAKE THE REIGNS OF STATE & MAKE THEM WORK AS THEIR OWN IN THE BEST INTERSTS OF THE PEOPLE, THEIR CHILDREN, THEIR FAMILIES AND GENERATIONS TO COME!

TABLE OF CONTENTS

Dedication

Acknowledgment

Authors' Foreword

———

ACKNOWLEDGMENT

To The COURAGE of John Jay Demonstrated At A Time Of Great Danger To Our Nation During Uncertain Times In American History.

Author's Foreword

I am reminded by history past the history of the United States would not be complete if it were not for those gallant men and women who in the face of danger, proceeded to do something Special about it! America's very existence is tied to her economic health which requires this generation understand & participate that being a citizen is more than thinking about it but knowing what to do about it that "frees" oneself to become the solution for our children & generations to come.

"Tyranny At The Waters' Edge: Draining The Swamp!"

Since the death of President Kennedy, events in America and the World have continued to show all of us how vulnerable our economic system is to currency manipulation and deficit spending by governments and the Congress of these United States, the result being a bloated deficit with borrowing and spending unaccountable to The Citizenry & States of these United States; including fiscal policies, laws and acts contrary to The BEST INTERESTS of ALL Americans. This is the ROOT of the social problems created within and by American society, fueled by OPPORTUNISTS, CARPETBAGGERS, USERS, MISUSERS & ABUSERS OF THE PEOPLE TO VOMENT DIVISION & CLASS WARFARE!

1. INTRODUCTION.

The *history of America* would not be complete if it were not for the men and women who sacrificed so much of themselves for a new nation and its children. Of course, much can be said of those who plotted against them and used them to profit at their expense. For those they must answer for us we must correct their mistakes for our children and generations to come. This then becomes the back ground and back drop of *TYRANNY AT THE WATERS' EDGE: "Draining The Swamp"*

"You cannot help the poor by destroying the Rich." "You cannot keep out of trouble by spending more than you earn." "You cannot lift the wage earner by pulling down the wage payer" – Abraham Lincoln

---

"I have always been afraid of banks."

"One man with courage makes a majority" "It is to be regretted that the rich and powerful too often bend the acts of government to their own selfish purposes." "Take time to deliberate but when the time for action arrives, stop thinking and go in." – *Andrew Jackson*

Let it be said, that America's finest hours are yet to come because the Children Of America can make a contribution to not only our Nation but also the World!

We are the product of generations past, present and future with the belief that our rights come from God; NOT THE STATE at a great cost to those who fought and died for them! That was the Social Contract created in 1781 at Yorktown-Gloucester Bay, Virginia.

The monuments laid at the reefs of those so honored are a testament to the sacrifice of so many for the hope that their sacrifice would *bear.* A proud nation was born and with it the greatest nation on earth in the history of man, *"AMERICA!"*

THE NATIONAL BACKGROUND

Early History

What was assumed by those in power was taken for granted by those struggling to live out their dreams. *AMERICA* was a land of opportunity because it's people made it their priority to continue living out their dreams for a better life for themselves and those for their children.

Colonial America grew at an astounding rate by the span of time from the founding of the Republic at Jamestown, Virginia 1607 until the last entry known as Georgia Colony 1732.

Of course, many events in between the time of founding and establishing Colonial life dominated the culture legally and politically;

particularly making it possible for 2.5 million people to realize their value because the Bible was read in the home, the schools and the Supreme Court! Ethics & Morales were also taught in the home practicing honesty and good business including honest services. The attitudes within the culture was fairness as the colonies grew in population and farming. As a result, the *Great Migration* ensued so that by the beginning of the War For Independence, *AMERICA* had enough population to fight England for it. And so we did on July 4, 1776 by way of the Declaration Of Independence, Congress, Philadelphia, Pennsylvania.

Now comes TYRANNY AT THE WATERS' EDGE redefining the current rules based on the *16th Amendment to the Constitution of these United States*. What does it say and what does it mean?

"*CONGRESS*, shall have power to lay

& collect taxes on incomes without regard to any census or enumeration. There was an income tax *prior* to this Amendment & it was in effect during Civil War." Ratified February 3, 1913

So, what we have here is a system of taxation based on representation of enumeration of census as to the number of folks occupy individual states. However, this Amendment did away with the census enumeration and went to a direct tax on income which now includes the Standard Deduction and deductions based on losses and gains. Could it be those with the most to lose tie themselves up with the government for as long as necessary to keep themselves from being penalized for surreptitious acts they commit during the period of doing their business? Therefore, no "free" lunch just tax

That is my point, unlike the history of *Early America* when life and government was much simpler and much smaller than now, we Americans did not have to deal with so much regulation and taxation without representation. Executive session was the oddity not common practice as is *today.*

And So, since President William Howard Taft, a man who held Office as both President and later as Chief Justice, history records his participation in the events that mark 1913 as a Turning point in American history.

Events do have a way of marking themselves to follow the outcome of what creates tremendous conflicts and tragedy in the lives of our Citizens and the outcome for our Children.

It is within this context that government *Of, By & For The People* will survive and thrive in this the twenty-first century and beyond.

We will need to understand how we got here and what we must do to preserve, protect & defend our liberty & freedom.

2. THE MEDIA

The honest truth is that America has become BIG Government at the expense of the Common man. They knew our economic health depended upon the strength of a strong dollar able to compete in the Global Market place unimpeded by fraud & schemes.

In Europe, the same holds true especially in the United Kingdom. Both The House Of Lords & The House Of Commons take their marching orders from the Queen of England closely administered by the Central Bank Of England.

That is how the International Monetary Fund & World Bank became the Central Banks of Europe by following policy from the Crown. All the other countries followed its lead and created what today is the European Union which ironically recently the UK withdrew by a vote of the people. To many

Brits, especially the Ruling Class, the EU has become an albatross around their necks by it's economic and political interests.

The Federal Reserve Act of 1913 set the stage for economic chaos not only for America but the entire World! Manipulation of currency laws in every country based on Central Bank policy has put the Bankers in control of the World; not THE PEOPLE!

Ok, so power & control by the bankers has displaced the American worker & their family.

There is a complete disconnect between what is *fair* and what is *just!* By making nations debtors to the Banks, the children & families suffer for lack of "equitable advantage". Laws that govern borrowing and spending create debt by which those in control benefit handsomely at the debtors expense which in many cases are families. More will be written about this subject as I lay out a plan to restore the family both economically and emotionally in their BEST INTERESTS for generations to come. So what does this have to do with the media?

The Act cemented in the minds of many Banks to administer the flow of currency and capital to their members. But again, the price was a Surrender of economic sovereignty to the banks which is the root of the problem in the World. "He that controls the Gold controls the Nation State", said Lord Cromwell. The *history* of the corruption does not stop there.

1913 was an interesting year for America not only for the signing by President Wilson but the ratification of the 16th Amendment by

The State Of Wyoming providing ¾ majority of states necessary to amend the Constitution.

The first IRS 1040 also rolled out to finance Wars as it continues today. The Banker's Cartel begins to roll since their secret meeting in 1910 on the Resort Jekyl Island, GA.

THE MEDIA PARTICIPATES!

How the 'Nation State' has survived is a testament to Providence in spite of years of abuse by forces foreign to the sacrifice & commitment of its Citizens.

But to a greater extent, the media is owned outright by those with the gold. He who owns the gold controls society. Once you study the history of America since Abraham Lincoln, you realize Americans have been set-up for failure by an elitist class of wealth driven thugs.

Their corruption has no limits, no bounds. conspiring together in 1910 on Jekyl Island, Georgia the bankers with the support of those in Congress devised a scheme by which the American people were deceived by stalking it's members with promises of better government financed by income taxes ruled unconstitutional in 1895 by the United States Supreme Court.

Since then with events to come, the country and our culture have been vulnerable to attack by different groups who's agenda to kill the Goose that lays the golden eggs, free-enterprise capitalism.

We must fight back by showing our resolve that economic freedom is synonymous with economic liberty; without both, we are Subjects of the State and rendered 'useful idiots', contrary to the to the Bill Of Rights and Constitution of these United States.

The abuse covers a lot of sins that have their origins in the pockets of the American people. With the income tax being established to pay interest on debt by Treasury, the stage was set to tax our wages and our profits in spite the Supreme Court said it unconstitutional on income from wages. By using the organs of the media, subversives are able to attack the very institutions that serve our citizens. This is treason and makes for a culture of despotism. That is where we are today.

But in a broader sense the abuse comprises those who have an aversion of subverting the Constitution designed to protect the American people from abusive government from within the government.

The other side are those forces outside the government wishing to take down the Republic by all means possible. These players are rooted in their own 'ism' "foreign" to our culture and work ethic of production and equity. Those groups must be exposed replaced by those who believe in Fairness & Rule of Law. The Media is complicit in these acts.

The policing mechanism on the Republic must come by The People themselves by becoming Citizen Candidates educated in that which works versus Generalities & Vagaries.

For this, I have authored several titles to fill the void. I will continue to speak about the plot to take down America witnessed best by those that knew & did something about it during their time. It is our duty to continue their legacy to fight & succeed against all threats both foreign & domestic including the three branches of government

3. PRESIDENT KENNEDY.

"The High Office Of The President Has Been Used To Foment A Plot To Destroy The Americans' Freedom & Before I Leave Office I Must Inform The Citizens Of This Plight".

President John Fitzgerald Kennedy, Columbia University November. 12, 1963.

What the President alluded to was the pernicious attitude upon the nation by the Cartel of International Bankers President Woodrow Wilson had signed into law a day prior to Christmas Eve December 23, 1913.

The Federal Reserve Act was a continuation of the financial abuse created upon the nation prior to its signing, in 1791 & 1816. Only Old Hickory shut down the Bank Of The United States in 1836 paying off the Federal Debt of $7,000,000.00 with The Federal Treasury. It still stands today.

Because of what the Banking Cartel had

done to the nation, President Kennedy was intent in undoing. Because the Federal Reserve Bank is a Central Bank its Charter exempted it from accountable oversight to any government entity. Its powers had to be reigned in.

John Kennedy made it his business to do just that by signing E.O. 11110 effectively transferring control of the Bank out of their hands to the United States Treasury. This in turn had the chilling effect of neutralizing the Bank's Charter putting it out of business. The Gold Standard still was backing US Dollar currency for The People.

Signed June 4, 1963, the Order provided for the printing of both Silver Certificates & United States Notes exempting the words Federal Reserve Note. Both bills showed their authenticity to the United States Treasury and were circulated prior to and shortly after President Kennedy's death November 22, 1963. That Order has never been rescinded but ignored by every

President since Kennedy. The National debt does not belong to the American People but to the private banking cartel known as the Federal Reserve Bank Of NY & its Branches!

Interest was exempt from the debt!

***** (for educational Art display only)*

RS - ($2.00 United States Note Circa 1963)

RS - ($5.00 United States Note Circa 1963)

*****(for   educational   Art   display   only)*

4. DOMESTIC SPYING

The Swamp is linked and comprises many players.

AS introduced during the Obama administration, Domestic Spying with or without Fisa Warrants.

Our first glimpse into it was when Edward Snowden downloaded a treasure trove of top secret documents showing that American Citizens are the target of government surveillance responsible for collecting & remitting the data collected to the United States Department Of Homeland Security.

This data is used to surveil citizens whom the government deems a threat upon their analytics of software they have perfected.

1. Transmissions listened to by analysts.

2. Emails analyzed by computer algorithms.

3. Word recognition analysis.

4. Electronic spying via cell phone data.

5. Devices that deviate from data collection.

Wikileaks has also contributed to the distrust created within the intelligence gathering agencies the American people pay for because they consider both Julian Assange Edward Snowden traitors yet provide a valuable service from the platforms they have created.

This author asks, "Would the DOJ, FBI NSA, CIA or any one of the 17 intelligence gathering agencies come clean what they were and are doing in the lives of the American people?" The answer is NO! they won't! They are sworn to secrecy and operate in stealth.

If we are to have an honest government we must establish trust in our servants. If they are not worthy of our trust, they must be replaced in toto. Each of the intelligent agencies are accountable to the American people by what they do and don't do.

The purpose of government is to protect its Citizens from threats to their property, lives money and Bill Of Rights; NOT TO GROW AN OUT OF CONTROL GOVT. AT THE EXPENSE OF ITS CITIZENS.

In my book "BALLONOMIC$: "Lifting America & The World Out Of Poverty From The Bottom Up", I discuss these issues & the investing in people making their lives secure both economically and personally.

In his book, 1984, George Orwell describes a society of surveillance on every street corner everyday creating a social environment of suspicion and anxiety. We have arrived at this threshold of stealth surveillance used to weaponize law enforcement agencies at the highest levels of government service to take down innocent people they disagree or dislike. It is a crisis.

5. SECURITY IND. SPECIALISTS

The Federal Government is undisciplined by design the case for the Swamp creatures that inhabit it. But in a greater sense it is a product of our time.

The attitudes and actions that American business created after World War II has contributed greatly including the link to the New World Order & decline of American sovereignty and stability.

Entitlements, Earmarks, Pork, Mandates, Gerrymandering and getting re-elected with few term limits have caused a burgeoning national debt and crisis of confidence in our nation's economy.

How much more can the nation endure until real change addresses the real problems of Income Inequality? Only time will tell, but in this author's humble opinion, it needs to start NOW!

Without exception, threats to the nations Security always has been a hot button issue because of the demands of government on The People. That stops NOW!

One can compare their own experience to everyday life of demands placed on our time and resources. So it is with problems created by government and an out-of-control undisciplined spending that causes harm to our nation and our lives.

To correct that requires more than wishful thinking. We must have a plan and make it a part of our national dialogue and life. "WE CAN!""WE WILL!" should be a slogan echoed in the Halls of Congress.

Our children will thank us for making it

and them our priority to secure their futures and those to come.

One such group known as the Security ustry Specialists, (SIS) formed by persons who use their positions undermine with tax payer dollars in the form of Pork, Earmarks, Mandates, Entitlements.

How many school lunch programs for little kids are we depriving by masking our true intentions in ways that hurt our nation and our Children?

On the streets of Washington D.C. I witnessed in 2012 homeless people and families sleeping on the streets and sides of buildings for not enough food to eat or a place to sleep. In a country as rich as these United States, I saw what poverty does to people and the aftermath of hopelessness makes. Skilled Labor prevents that social experience of homelessness. Making life affordable is the challenge we face and it starts with the budget economy that works for all Americans and their families. From there, Citizenship becomes the responsibility of us all to see our children are educated and our community productive. Skilled labor solves a multitude of problems politicians create and ignore at the people's expense.

But the problems morph into other areas hell bent in destroying our society for ill gotten gains. Security Industry Specialists in Seattle, Washington is being accused of being a front organization to that goal. It is alleged by some, that George Soros, Bill Gates, Henry Kessinger, NWO, Clinton Foundation, DNC, CIA, ABA infiltrating the Federal government in all three branches military and Higher Education.

With terrorist groups like ANTIFA inciting civil violence at the expense of law and order, the Swamp continues to show it's ugly reality to law abiding citizens. Poking the eye of the bear is not a good idea when those who serve our military and those who served our nation, come in the cross hairs of such events.

Nothing good can come out of violent Confrontations but the deaths of those who Harbor violence in their hearts toward other People for a variety of reasons. Politics like history, is full of instances by which power and control of the masses is the ultimate goal of the leadership. We must find a better way to lead & guide our nation for people.

6. DOJ, FBI, CIA, NSA, COURTS.

"Our Problems As A Nation Is An Electorate Given To Fraud & Abuse"

The investigations by Congress into the 2016 email scandals Clinton campaign puts blame on several parties adverse to America.

These parties reflect the title of this page and cause concern as to their legitimacy as institutions operating at taxpayer expense within these United States.

It is alleged that these agencies reflect a conspiracy by senior level executives to cause injury within their departments by subverting the rules for their interests as a group following their own agenda. Abuse of their power is cause for concern and puts them & the American people at risk. Since the death of President Kennedy & the creation of these government agencies, our liberty and freedoms have been greatly diminished particularly since 9/11.

DOJ

<u>DEPARTMENT OF JUSTICE</u>

Since the events that have marked the Election of 2016, the Department of Justice participated in crimes against the United States by failing to prosecute parties shown to have broken the law and cause injury to our society.

Our history also shows that since 1913, *America* has failed to put in place safeguards to prevent this unaccountable cycle to come to an END!. WE THE PEOPLE, demand that this government stop it's endless cycle for the good of our Country, our Children and Generations to come!

The Swamp Creatures within the DOJ have been identified. Many of them are part of the Council of 500 which come from the Senior Executive Services. Those folks are middle managers unaccountable sitting between cabinet level positions and G15 status, the highest grade of Civil Service.

Many at "Justice" prescribe themselves to an attitude of entitlement because they are the 'elite' of the DC beltway setting a very bad example to fellow colleagues regarding the rule of law and consequences to those who use & violate it for their personal gain.

There are many examples in the last eight years when the Obama administration made several errors of legal ease that implicated

high level officials within the DOJ & FBI.

One who comes to mind is that of Lanny

Davis, an Assistant Attorney General who

spent years covering for crimes by others

within the department. How do we know?

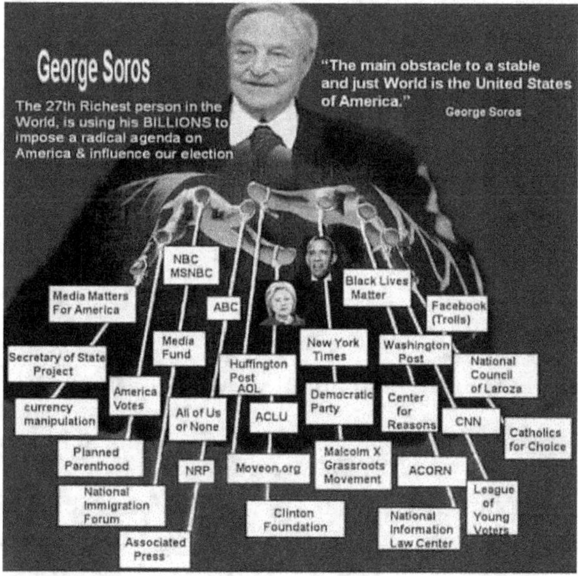

This author personally has been chasing

bad actors for years in attempt to recover

from damages caused at the State level to his family and particularly his mother. The result that discovery is made how corrupt State & Federal Government is to its own people.

However, this plays well in seeking justice not only for his family but also for every American child born into this unacceptable rotten vortex of financial illegal exploitation of the family both State & Federal. These are the real Swamp Creatures in America.

Decisions that are at that level impact all of us because they send a message of what is acceptable and what isn't. The Obama era & to a greater extent, the Clinton & Bush era made a precedent of allowing abusive govt.

to become the norm in America. The Swamp

is teeming to be Drained!

The Cartel of bad government reaches farther than we know. The titling of this comprises the agencies most responsible for the decline of the nation while the American people are being attacked by its Government. How is it going to Stop?

First, the restoration of the financial system is long over due for a complete overhaul. In my book THE FAIR DEAL, I discuss the relationship that evolved over decades of corrupt government policy in the last century.

Over a hundred years have gone since the Signing of the Federal Reserve Act, 1913. That event has caused this nation and world a great deal of anxiety relative to economic policy because from the beginning it was make the "System" work for them opposite the American Taxpayer.

In effect, it is a corrupt institution that Funds the International Monetary Fund & The World Bank.

There is absolutely no evidence that Executive Order 11110 signed June 4, 1963 has been rescinded or the wording that nullified it despite other President's issues.

We are left that since every President since Lyndon Johnson, has ignored it that perhaps fearful that if they were to follow its directive, they too might be killed. Both Lincoln and Kennedy believed the *Nation* should issue and regulate its own currency, not a foreign bank masquerading around as a Federal entity but a private banking cartel.

The nation had seen this before during

the presidency of Andrew Jackson (1829-1837).

THE BANK OF THE UNITED STATES was shut down by Jackson but an attempt was made on his life. Jackson, founder of the Democratic Party surmised as warned by George Washington that the currency of the nation was sovereign to the United States Treasury and should stay in its control both in the manufacturing and minting of printed and coined currency.

The inflation non-backed currency wars on the dollar devaluing the dollars' worth in terms of purchasing power and payment of debt release. Diluting the economy with unbacked green backs is a recipe for more inflation and higher prices.

Backed securities with Gold or Silver

makes for a much more stable economy disallowing the government from over spending and causing families harm by a reckless and selfish policy of greed.

REAL CAPITALISM will cause the Federal government to shrink because it will no longer be able to control a rogue policy of self-enrichment at the expense of the taxpayers and their families. The Federal government will have to learn to live within its means like Citizens must live within a budget. The Charter Bank will replace the Central Bank aka Federal Reserve System.

The boom and bust cycles in the *history* of the nation is over. Economic prosperity for America will be measured in real dollars backed by Gold or Silver instead of nothing!

The national debt will be gone and the

dawning of a new era in funding will begin! War bonds, Saving Bonds, Treasury Bills all have their place raising money for worthy Causes and Investments for the The People!

The Shadow government that controls our nation must be gone. The bureaucrats unaccountable to The People must GO!

FBI, NSA, CIA, COURTS

Once respected now rejected by the American people. Having betrayed their role in government, their reputations morphed into self-serving institutions of power and control into the lives of their Citizens.

Fed up, the American people have said, "NO MORE!" The People demand a new Government, one accountable to them, and their families. Policies that create & support living wages, fair taxes & free-enterprise.

7. ORGANIZING FOR ACTION (OFA)

Standing only four miles from the former residence of Barack Obama on Belmont Rd. NW is the home of the OFA. Their goal to disrupt & disarm the current Presidency of Donald J. Trump. Given to the doctrine that the ends justify the means, they number in the thousands all over the country. They are also known as Obama's Army in Chicago.

It came to be three days after his Oath taking January 23, 2009 and has evolved since. Known in all 50 States, Obama has made it his objective to advance progressive Socialistic ideology contrary to Founders beliefs of a strong unified Constitutional Republican government ruled by law for the benefit of traditional families & her people.

Since its founding, Obama has used it to

to advance his agenda to fight traditional values introducing non-traditional ideas that hijack and undercut the ability of the traditional family to survive and thrive abandoning their dependence on government programs reducing dependence on taxes.

In addition, Obama stocked the Senior Executive Services with ten thousand Interim managers sitting under cabinet level Executives but above G15 pay grade Civil Servants.

Again the goal for these people to disrupt and cause injury to our country & those in positions to reverse the damage caused by years of abuse by the past administration.

This was and is Obama's legacy. No President ever engaged in this treachery for President Woodrow Wilson that led us to war and began the down hill economic progression that has led us to where we are today.

Consistent throughout all the proceedings & events leading up to the period of Obama were events that caused him to form ties with groups associated with the Muslim Brotherhood.

Valarie Jarrett, Susan Rice contributed greatly the infiltration of unaccountable government officials in key places of the administration of Barack Hussein Obama II.

Obama supported the Council on Islamic Relations, CAIR and provided member dues in the amounts of $100,000.00 annually. The federal government is a thorn in the side of the American People. It must be drained of its sewage and remodeled for our people.

8. ADULT GUARDIANSHIP

As in the case of spending & borrowing by the federal government, there is nothing regulating it in the Constitution. It appears a Conundrum exists of legal v. illegal acts by those engaged in using a position of trust to to feather themselves at our expense & to cause personal injury to our loved ones.

This is consistent in adult guardianship. Being hijacked from your home is common and unacceptable destroying the life estate a couple built to pass on to their children. By the actions of Probate Judges, lawyers, doctors, guardians, nursing home staff, the crisis grows into an epidemic. It must Stop!

Not one governor of any State has come out against the exploitation of the elderly by Court officials who betray their Oath &

allow their offices to be used to further the interests of Nursing Home lobbyists & those seeking reelection for campaign funding and contributions. Power & control of Citizens is the name of their game falling outside the boundaries established by the Constitution and rule of law.

Adult guardianship as a weapon to rob and steal one's property & assets by stealth is a practice introduced during American slavery where slaves were trafficked through the Courts as chattel property.

This practice was barbaric and eventually banned by the 13th Amendment, its remnants are still with us taking on the form of human ownership through Probate guardianship; the same system used during the slave trade.

What do we have to do to tame this

Swamp Monster? First, we must identify the problem. What is it? Then mobilize for action. The history of the United States has always been built by those who know what they know to be true and do something about it. It is no different today. Action!

What had created the conflicts that led to War with the British at the founding of the Republic? The greed of the British elite!

To some, to have it shoved down the throats of the electorate is tantamount to treason. President Kennedy knew and saw what an out-of-control government would look like and put in place "acts" to bring a plausible sustainable result to years of abuse upon the banking and finance system and ultimately the abuse upon the American taxpayer.

 Big government both in terms of its military and intelligence gathering apparatus causes all our citizens concern when the funding of these departments and agencies go rogue on THE PEOPLE. We as a People and America as a nation, have a duty to correct that threatens our safety and economic security. It is in that context reforms are needed to reverse the trends that currently operate within local, State & Federal governments demanding a change that will correct years of abuse by those who have allowed it.

ADULT GUARDIANSHIP are the new Slave courts run by misfit Judges, Lawyers Guardians, Hospitals causing harm and Stealing family inheritances. It is a tragedy THAT DEMANDS OUR ATTENTION!

The Deep State unlike the Shadow government comprises of the Industrial Military complex according to Kevin Shipp.

Kevin was a former CIA Operative who like Julian Assange & Edward Snowden making known the goings on of the New World Order, Federal Reserve Banking Cartels and the schemes being created to defeat freedom for encampment of death.

Adult guardianship is one of them. Not enough has been told by mainstream media to show the horrific damage Americans suffer by it. Is this the next holocaust?

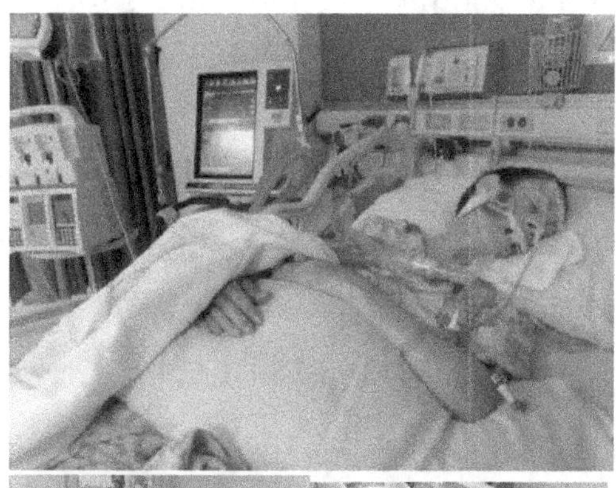

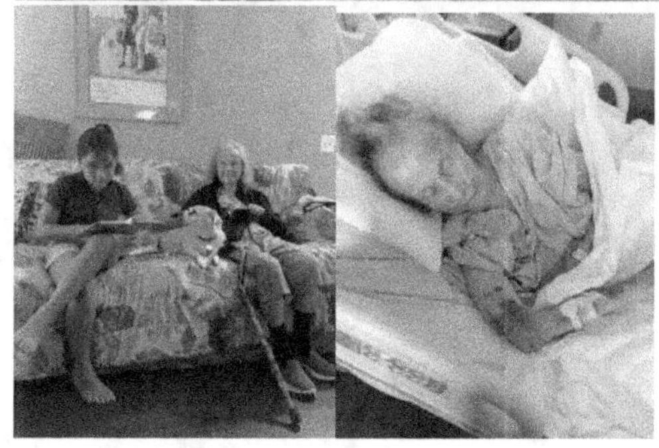

9. STATE CPS/FOSTER CARE

Years of economic policies creating mass chaos within market conditions are based on the notion that profits trump the BEST INTERESTS of people, particularly those with the ability to exploit others for personal gain. That policy exists today.

THE BALL DOCTRINE points out the absolute need to *reign-in* the money powers that have created so much harm to so many people throughout World History. This was President Kennedy's vision:

'He believed the family *reigned supreme* as the basic social unit of every nation'.

Speech after speech, the affirmations of America's global supremacy over those nation's who created harm to the national security of the United States and its foreign policy directives were met head on by the Kennedy administration. Kennedy was a man of *destiny* and his policies created serious challenges for the establishment.

To that end, I have attempted to show what is lacking in the economic health of the nation. Central banks cause harm in the modern world because their policies are corrupted from within by policies created in 1910 and beyond starting at *Jekyl Island, Georgia.*

What is needed now is an act that corrects and cancels the harm that began over 100 years ago.

'THE BALL ACT' makes it possible. Conceived in *Liberty*, the act affirms the treason of Woodrow Wilson signing the

Federal Reserve Act on December 23, 1913 while Congress was out of session during Christmas.

A progressive, he violated his Oath of Office as President allowing enemies of The People to exploit the Constitution! As long as Central Banks could charge the federal government interest on non-backed money, the corrupt establishment allowed it to pass. President Kennedy knew the Constitutional Powers of Separation of the three branches of government and that in effect it was the United States Treasury should be in control of America's *monetary and currency policy.*

This violation of America's sovereignty showed Kennedy what previous Presidents also knew: 'The issuing of money was to come through Congress; not a Central Bank!

In 1997, Hillary Clinton lobbied Congress to pass the Adoption & Safe Families Act, signed into law November 19, 1997. Amended Title IV-E Social Security Administration.

The law was used as a ruse to steal Children from good families & reward States financially and foster parents for These unlawful and evil acts.

As a result, America's children are traumatized by a rogue regime & schemes. This is not what the founders wanted or envisioned.

Now it is twenty-one years later and things are very bad within the States. Child trafficking, drug addiction, mental illness reign supreme at the expense of our kids and their parents. It is a holocaust must stop!

The Fabian Communists came to America at the turn of the Twentieth Century by stealth and weaseled their way into academia while the Banking Cartel made their way into the financial system of The United States leading to the Great Depression.

The damage done to Society is so great that it will require major changes in every facet of government to restore the public trust.

No child should be deprived of their parents and family. The Courts sustain it causing more damage for the nation and for its children. This is immoral, unlawful using taxpayer to reward the theft of our children. This must stop by Citizen participation repealing this law!

10. DEA & DRUG CARTELS

CAPITALISM takes on the nation and the world, The People will be vilified. Years of abuse by an intrusive and corrupt system of swindle and scandal will finally be gone never to return.

The Federal Reserve System has its Tentacles in the International Monetary Fund (IMF) and the World Bank (WB).

Every nation is vulnerable to the Central Bank policy of *fiat capital* like problems it creates in Greece & Venezuela.

The Bankers have created a fail proof System of banking that works for them at expense of their depositors. By weakening the dollar through dumping dollars into the market, *Inflation* results with more dollars to pay for essential goods and services in relationship to the nation's Gross National Product (GNP). President Kennedy was all over it and knew that it could bankrupt the country; something he wanted to prevent!

I believe Robert Kennedy had he become President would have continued the policies his older brother created.

Both Kennedy brothers knew that War & Money corrupt a country. Both were against the exploitation of both. That is what the bankers wanted tied to The Federal Reserve System. From it, it can be conjectured that David Rockefeller and his Tri-lateral Commission & Council of Foreign Relations have directly benefited from the power the bankers have created by this debt creating system of *fiat capital*.

The relationship be

tween capital and drugs has a sorted past. BigPharma is dependent on capital expenditures to provide necessary resources to experiment in research & development (R&D) of products that provide relief for specific problems.

However, the abuse of these products do produce addictions that kill. The opioid drug crisis created by overseas pharmaceutical giants flooding the United States is a result of greed by their producers. It is now a crisis threatening our nation and culture.

But it doesn't stop there. Crystal Methanfedomine, Crack Cocaine, Heroine, Methadone, Antibiotics, Marijuana, LSD, Pain Killers are all addictive drugs that cause harm to the families of those they impact.

These are addictive drugs. The Drug Enforcement Agency (DEA) is charged with safeguarding the nation from abusive and addictive criminal enterprises preying on the Citizenry.

There is a web of deception the Cartels created for suppliers and users to avoid detection. But the drug problem is causing death in the population at our expense. Their tactics are stealthy & deceptive for their suppliers and dealers.

The DEA is responsible with other intelligence agencies to work to STOP the proliferation of these drugs. But to a greater degree any drug can be abused if not monitored by one's doctor and their pharmacist. Dangerous drugs seem to make their way into the mainstream. Young people experimenting mixing hard drugs can kill them. Older adults can too causing the break up of their families and children.

Emotional insecurity causes people much pain but drugs don't solve the problem. God does. Our families and our children deserve better & society has an obligation to protect them.

Gangs proliferate around the drug culture where communities allow it. Violence is a product of that too resulting in death. The breakdown of society can be traced to events caused by a lack of family participation. Out hope is to make strong families by creating accountable government; economic support.

This is the challenging part our people must participate to support our children

11. THE CONGRESS

As you can see in the picture those in the Congress sitting during the standing for the "Pledge Of Allegiance" to the Flag shows a tremendous disrespect for our system of government and disrespect to those who died to defend it.

As far as this author is concerned, all of these of people should be removed from the Congress of the United States. Representing their districts is an honor that they dishonor by their contempt for our people.

They are not a law unto themselves but Public servants paid with taxpayer dollars supporting them and their staffs with a lifestyle most Americans will never know.

They are the Swamp that must be drained. Citizens must jump in to correct this aspect of Representative Government.

12. MUELLER INVESTIGATION

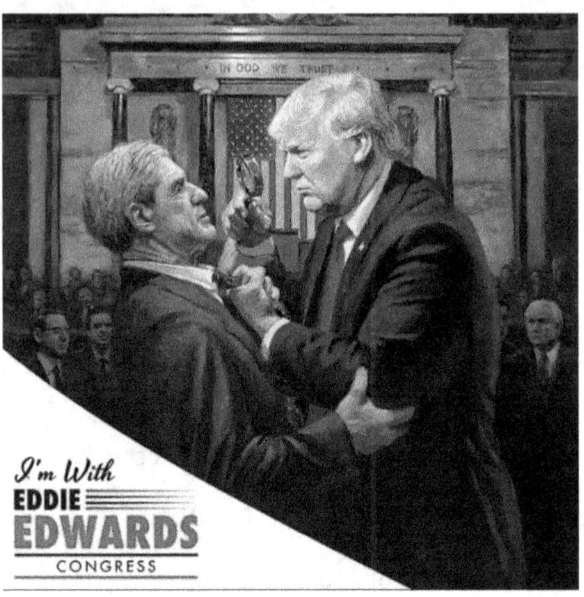

Robert Mueller was appointed as a Special Counsel to investigate allegations of Russian collusion in the 2016 Presidential election of Donald Trump.

However, what has come of it is an exercise known as a Hegel Dialectic.

That is, an exercise in propaganda pointing the finger back at Mueller and his staff of lawyers.

Rightfully so, President Donald Trump has a beef with the investigation because it appears it is set up to remove him.

Mueller's appointment as Special Counsel is unconstitutional because he was appointed by Assistant United States Attorney General Rod Rosenstein after United States Attorney General Jeff Session, recused himself from the investigation of a fake dossier paid by the Clinton campaign.

This is the problem of a central Government without controls and accountability. The good news is that the players who have committed all the dirt are being tarred with their own brush.

Tyranny At The Waters Edge shows how corrupt our society became over 100 years and what must be done to drain the Swamp to make it safe again.

<u>APPENDIX</u>

The first fiscal year for the U.S. Government started Jan. 1, 1789. Congress changed the beginning of the fiscal year from Jan. 1 to Jul. 1 in 1842, and finally from Jul. 1 to Oct. 1 in 1977 where it remains today.

Date	Dollar Amount
07/01/1849	63,061,858.69
07/01/1848	47,044,862.23
07/01/1847	38,826,534.77
07/01/1846	15,550,202.97
07/01/1845	15,925,303.01
07/01/1844	23,461,652.50
07/01/1843	32,742,922.00
01/01/1843	20,201,226.27
01/01/1842	13,594,480.73
01/01/1841	5,250,875.54
01/01/1840	3,573,343.82
01/01/1839	10,434,221.14
01/01/1838	3,308,124.07
01/01/1837	336,957.83

01/01/1836	37,513.05
01/01/1835	33,733.05
01/01/1834	4,760,082.08
01/01/1833	7,001,698.83
01/01/1832	24,322,235.18
01/01/1831	39,123,191.68
01/01/1830	48,565,406.50
01/01/1829	58,421,413.67
01/01/1828	67,475,043.87
01/01/1827	73,987,357.20
01/01/1826	81,054,059.99
01/01/1825	83,788,432.71
01/01/1824	90,269,777.77
01/01/1823	90,875,877.28
01/01/1822	93,546,676.98
01/01/1821	89,987,427.66
01/01/1820	91,015,566.15
01/01/1819	95,529,648.28
01/01/1818	103,466,633.83
01/01/1817	123,491,965.16
01/01/1816	127,334,933.74
01/01/1815	99,833,660.15
01/01/1814	81,487,846.24

01/01/1813	55,962,827.57
01/01/1812	45,209,737.90
01/01/1811	48,005,587.76
01/01/1810	53,173,217.52
01/01/1809	57,023,192.09
01/01/1808	65,196,317.97
01/01/1807	69,218,398.64
01/01/1806	75,723,270.66
01/01/1805	82,312,150.50
01/01/1804	86,427,120.88
01/01/1803	77,054,686.40
01/01/1802	80,712,632.25
01/01/1801	83,038,050.80
01/01/1800	82,976,294.35
01/01/1799	78,408,669.77
01/01/1798	79,228,529.12
01/01/1797	82,064,479.33
01/01/1796	83,762,172.07
01/01/1795	80,747,587.39
01/01/1794	78,427,404.77
01/01/1793	80,358,634.04
01/01/1792	77,227,924.66
01/01/1791	75,463,476.52

01/01/1790	71,060,508.50

President Kennedy, The Fed And Executive Order 11110

From APFN

By Cedric X

11-20-3

Executive Order 1110 gave the US the ability to create its own money backed by silver. ...

http://www.john-f-kennedy.net/executiveorder11110.htm

On June 4, 1963, a little known attempt was made to strip the Federal Reserve Bank of its power to loan money to the government at interest. On that day President John F. Kennedy signed Executive Order No. 11110 that returned to the U.S. government the power to issue currency, without going through the Federal Reserve. Mr. Kennedy's order gave the Treasury the power "to issue silver certificates against any silver bullion, silver, or standard silver dollars in the Treasury." This meant that for every ounce of silver in the U.S. Treasury's vault, the government could introduce new money into circulation. In all, Kennedy brought nearly $4.3 billion in U.S. notes into circulation. The ramifications of this bill are enormous.

With the stroke of a pen, Mr. Kennedy was on his way to putting the Federal Reserve Bank of New York out of business. If enough of these silver certificates were to come into circulation they would have eliminated the demand for Federal Reserve notes. This is because the silver certificates are backed by silver and the Federal Reserve notes are not backed by anything. Executive Order 11110 could have prevented the national debt from reaching its current level, because it would have given the government the ability to repay its debt without going to the Federal Reserve and being charged interest in order to create the new money. Executive Order 11110 gave the U.S. the ability to create its own money backed by silver.

After Mr. Kennedy was assassinated just five months later, no more silver certificates were issued. The Final Call has learned that the Executive Order was never repealed by any U.S. President through an Executive Order and is still valid. Why then has no president utilized it? Virtually all of the nearly $6 trillion in debt has been created since 1963, and if a U.S. president had utilized Executive Order 11110 the debt would be nowhere near the current level.

Perhaps the assassination of JFK was a warning to future presidents who would think to eliminate the U.S. debt by eliminating the Federal Reserve's control over the creation of money. Mr. Kennedy challenged the government of money by challenging the two most successful vehicles that have ever been used to drive up debt - war and the creation of money by a privately-owned central bank. His efforts to have all troops out of Vietnam by 1965 and Executive Order 11110 would have severely cut into the profits and control of the New York banking establishment. As America's debt reaches unbearable levels and a conflict emerges in Bosnia that will further increase America's debt, one is force to ask, will President Clinton have the courage to consider utilizing Executive Order 11110 and, if so, is he willing to pay the ultimate price for doing so?

Executive Order 11110 AMENDMENT OF EXECUTIVE ORDER NO. 10289

AS AMENDED, RELATING TO THE PERFORMANCE OF CERTAIN FUNCTIONS AFFECTING THE DEPARTMENT OF THE TREASURY

By virtue of the authority vested in me by section 301 of title 3 of the United States Code, it is ordered as follows:

Section 1. Executive Order No. 10289 of September 19, 1951, as amended, is hereby further amended-

By adding at the end of paragraph 1 thereof the following subparagraph (j):

(j) The authority vested in the President by paragraph (b) of section 43 of the Act of May 12,1933, as amended (31 U.S.C.821(b)), to issue silver certificates against any silver bullion, silver, or standard silver dollars in the Treasury not then held for redemption of any outstanding silver certificates, to prescribe the denomination of such silver certificates, and to coin standard silver dollars and subsidiary silver currency for their redemption

and --

By revoking subparagraphs (b) and (c) of paragraph 2 thereof.

Sec. 2. The amendments made by this Order shall not affect any act done, or any right accruing or accrued or any suit or proceeding had or commenced in any civil or criminal cause prior to the date of this Order but all such liabilities shall continue and may be enforced as if said amendments had not been made.

 John F. Kennedy The White House, June 4, 1963.

Of course, the fact that both JFK and Lincoln met the the same end is a mere coincidence.

Abraham Lincoln's Monetary Policy, 1865 (Page 91 of Senate document 23.)

Money is the creature of law and the creation of the original issue of money should be maintained as the exclusive monopoly of national Government.

Money possesses no value to the State other than that given to it by circulation.

Capital has its proper place and is entitled to every protection. The wages of men should be recognized in the structure of and in the social order as more important than the wages of money.

No duty is more imperative for the Government than the duty it owes the People to furnish them with a sound and uniform currency, and of regulating the circulation of the medium of exchange so that labor will be protected from a vicious currency, and commerce will be facilitated by cheap and safe exchanges.

The available supply of Gold and Silver being wholly inadequate to permit the issuance of coins of intrinsic value or paper currency convertible into coin in the volume required to serve the needs of the People, some other basis for the issue of currency must be developed, and some means other than that of convertibility into coin must be developed to prevent undue fluctuation in the value of paper currency or any other substitute for money of intrinsic value that may come into use.

The monetary needs of increasing numbers of People advancing towards higher standards of living can and should be met by the Government. Such needs can be served by the issue of National Currency and Credit through the operation of a National Banking system .The circulation of a medium of exchange issued and backed by the Government can be properly regulated and redundancy of issue avoided by withdrawing from circulation such amounts as may be necessary by Taxation, Redeposit, and otherwise. Government has the power to regulate the currency and credit of the Nation.

Government should stand behind its currency and credit and the Bank deposits of the Nation. No individual should suffer a loss of money through depreciation or inflated currency or Bank bankruptcy.

Government possessing the power to create and issue currency and creditas money and enjoying the right to withdraw both currency and credit from circulation by Taxation and otherwise need not and should not borrow capital at interest as a means of financing Governmental work and public enterprise. The Government should create, issue, and circulate all the currency and credit needed to satisfy the spending power of the Government and the buying power of the consumers. The privilege of creating and issuing money is not only the supreme prerogative of Government, but it is the Governments greatest creative opportunity.

By the adoption of these principles the long felt want for a uniform medium will be satisfied. The taxpayers will be saved immense sums of interest, discounts, and exchanges. The financing of all public enterprise, the maintenance of stable Government and ordered progress, and the conduct of the Treasury will become matters of practical administration. The people can and will be furnished with a currency as safe as their own Government. Money will cease to be master and become the servant of humanity. Democracy will rise superior to the money power.

Some information on the Federal Reserve The Federal Reserve, a Private Corporation One of the most common concerns among people who engage in any effort to reduce their taxes is, "Will keeping my money hurt the government's ability to pay it's bills?" As explained in the first article in this series, the modern withholding tax does not, and wasn't designed to, pay for government services. What it does do, is pay for the privately-owned Federal Reserve System.

Black's Law Dictionary defines the "Federal Reserve System" as, "Network of twelve central banks to which most national banks belong and to which state chartered banks may belong. Membership rules require investment of stock and minimum reserves."

Privately-owned banks own the stock of the Fed. This was explained in more detail in the case of Lewis v. United States, Federal Reporter, 2nd Series, Vol. 680, Pages 1239, 1241 (1982), where the court said:

Each Federal Reserve Bank is a separate corporation owned by commercial banks in its region. The stockholding commercial banks elect two thirds of each Bank's nine member board of directors.

Similarly, the Federal Reserve Banks, though heavily regulated, are locally controlled by their member banks. Taking another look at Black's Law Dictionary, we find that these privately owned banks actually issue money:

Federal Reserve Act. Law which created Federal Reserve banks which act as agents in maintaining money reserves, issuing money in the form of bank notes, lending money to banks, and supervising banks. Administered by Federal Reserve Board (q.v.).

The FED banks, which are privately owned, actually issue, that is, create, the money we use. In 1964 the House Committee on Banking and Currency, Subcommittee on Domestic Finance, at the second session of the 88th Congress, put out a study entitled Money Facts which contains a good description of what the FED is:

The Federal Reserve is a total money-making machine. It can issue money or checks. And it never has a problem of making its checks good because it can obtain the $5 and $10 bills necessary to cover its check simply by asking the Treasury Department's Bureau of Engraving to print them.

As we all know, anyone who has a lot of money has a lot of power. Now imagine a group of people who have the power to create money. Imagine the power these people would have. This is what the Fed is.

No man did more to expose the power of the Fed than Louis T. McFadden, who was the Chairman of the House Banking Committee back in the 1930s. Constantly pointing out that monetary issues shouldn't be partisan, he criticized both the Herbert Hoover and Franklin Roosevelt administrations. In describing the Fed, he remarked in the Congressional Record, House pages 1295 and 1296 on June 10, 1932, that:

Mr. Chairman, we have in this country one of the most corrupt institutions the world has ever known. I refer to the Federal Reserve Board and the Federal reserve banks. The Federal Reserve Board, a Government Board, has cheated the Government of the United States and he people of the United States out of enough money to pay the national debt. The depredations and the iniquities of the Federal Reserve Board and the Federal reserve banks acting together have cost this country enough money to pay the national debt several times over. This evil institution has impoverished and ruined the people of the United States; has bankrupted itself, and has practically bankrupted our Government. It has done this through the maladministration of that law by which the Federal Reserve Board, and through the corrupt practices of the moneyed vultures who control it.

Some people think the Federal reserve banks are United States Government institutions. They are not Government institutions. They are private credit monopolies which prey upon the people of the United States for the benefit of themselves and their foreign customers; foreign and domestic speculators and swindlers; and rich and predatory money lenders. In that dark crew of financial pirates there are those who would cut a man's throat to get a dollar out of his pocket; there are those who send money into States to buy votes to control our legislation; and there are those who maintain an international propaganda for the purpose of deceiving us and of wheedling us into the granting of new concessions which will permit them to cover up their past misdeeds and set again in motion their gigantic train of crime. Those 12 private credit monopolies were deceitfully and disloyally foisted upon this country by bankers who came here from Europe and who repaid us for our hospitality by undermining our American institutions.

The Fed basically works like this: The government granted its power to create money to the Fed banks. They create money, then loan it back to the government charging interest. The government levies income taxes to pay the interest on the debt. On this point, it's interesting to note that the Federal Reserve act and the sixteenth amendment, which gave congress the power to collect income taxes, were both passed in 1913. The incredible power of the Fed over the economy is universally admitted. Some people, especially in the banking and academic communities, even support it. On the other hand, there are those, both in the past and in the present, that speak out against it. One of these men was President John F. Kennedy. His efforts were detailed in Jim Marrs' 1990 book, Crossfire:

Another overlooked aspect of Kennedy's attempt to reform American society involves money. Kennedy apparently reasoned that by returning to the constitution, which states that only Congress shall coin and regulate money, the soaring national debt could be reduced by not paying interest to the bankers of the Federal Reserve System, who print paper money then loan it to the government at interest. He moved in this area on June 4, 1963, by signing Executive Order 11,110 which called for the issuance of $4,292,893,815 in United States Notes through the U.S. Treasury rather than the traditional Federal Reserve System. That same day, Kennedy signed a bill changing the backing of one and two dollar bills from silver to gold, adding strength to the weakened U.S. currency.

Kennedy's comptroller of the currency, James J. Saxon, had been at odds with the powerful Federal Reserve Board for some time, encouraging broader investment and lending powers for banks that were not part of the Federal Reserve system. Saxon also had decided that non-Reserve banks could underwrite state and local general obligation bonds, again weakening the dominant Federal Reserve banks.

A number of "Kennedy bills" were indeed issued - the author has a five dollar bill in his possession with the heading "United States Note" - but were quickly withdrawn after Kennedy's death. According to information from the Library of the Comptroller of the Currency, Executive Order 11,110 remains in effect today, although successive administrations beginning with that of President Lyndon Johnson apparently have simply ignored it and instead returned to the practice of paying interest on Federal Reserve notes. Today we continue to use Federal Reserve Notes, and the deficit is at an all-time high.

The point being made is that the IRS taxes you pay aren't used for government services. It won't hurt you, or the nation, to legally reduce or eliminate your tax liability.

From The Final Call, Vol15, No.6, on January 17, 1996 (USA)

<http://www.apfn.org/apfn/eo11110.pdf>http://www.apfn.org/apfn/eo11110.pdf

http://disc.server.com/discussion.cgi?disc=149495;article=46736;title=APFN

JFK vs. Federal Reserve

On June 4, 1963, a virtually unknown Presidential decree, Executive Order 11110, was signed by President John Fitzgerald Kennedy with the intention to strip the Federal Reserve Bank of its power to loan money to the United States Federal Government at interest. With the stroke of a pen, President Kennedy declared that the privately owned Federal Reserve Bank would soon be out of business. This matter has been exhaustively researched by the Christian Common Law Institute through the Federal Register and Library of Congress, and the Institute has conclude that President Kennedy's Executive Order has never been repealed, amended, or superceded by any subsequent Executive Order. In simple terms, it is still valid.

When John Fitzgerald Kennedy, author of Profiles in Courage, signed this Order, it returned to the federal government, specifically to the Treasury Department, the Constitutional power to create and issue currency -- money -- without going through the privately owned Federal Reserve Bank. President Kennedy's Executive Order 11110 gave the Treasury Department the explicit authority: "to issue silver certificates against any silver bullion, silver, or standard silver dollars in the Treasury" [the full text is displayed below]. This means that for every ounce of silver in the U.S. Treasury's vault, the government could introduce new money into circulation based on the silver bullion physically held therein. As a result, more than $4 billion in United States Notes were brought into circulation in $2 and $5 denominations. Although $10 and $20 United States Notes were never circulated, they were being printed by the Treasury Department when Kennedy was assassinated.

Certainly it's obvious that President Kennedy knew that the Federal Reserve Notes being circulated as "legal currency" were contrary to the Constitution of the United States, which calls for issuance of "United States Notes" as interest-free and debt-free currency backed by silver reserves in the U.S. Treasury. Comparing a "Federal Reserve Note" issued from the private central bank of the United States (i.e., the Federal Reserve Bank a/k/a Federal Reserve System), with a "United States Note" from the U.S. Treasury (as issued by President Kennedy's Executive Order), the two almost look alike, except one says "Federal

Reserve Note" on the top while the other says "United States Note". In addition, the Federal Reserve Note has a green seal and serial number while the United States Note has a red seal and serial number. Following President Kennedy's assassination on November 22, 1963, the United States Notes he had issued were immediately taken out of circulation, and Federal Reserve Notes continued to serve as the "legal currency" of the nation.

Kennedy knew that if the silver-backed United States Notes were widely circulated, they would eliminated the demand for Federal Reserve Notes. This is a simple matter of economics. USNs were backed by silver and FRNs were (still are) backed by nothing of intrinsic value. As a result of Executive Order 11110, the national debt would have prevented from reaching its current level (almost all of the $9 trillion in federal debt has been created since 1963). Executive Order 11110 also granted the U.S. Government the power to repay past debt without further borrowing from the privately owned Federal Reserve which charged both principle and interest and all new "money" it "created." Finally, Executive Order 11110 gave the U.S.A. the ability to create its own money backed by silver, again giving money real value.

Perhaps President Kennedy's assassination was a warning to future presidents not to interfere with the private Federal Reserve's control over the creation of money. For, with true courage, JFK had boldly challenged the two most successful vehicles that have ever been used to drive up debt: 1) war (i.e., the Vietnam war); and, 2) the creation of money by a privately owned central bank. His efforts to have all U.S. troops out of Vietnam by 1965 combined with Executive Order 11110 would have destroyed the profits and control of the private Federal Reserve Bank.

Executive Order 11110, the AMENDMENT of EXECUTIVE ORDER No. 10289, as amended RELATING to the PERFORMANCE of CERTAIN FUNCTIONS AFFECTING the DEPARTMENT of the TREASURY:

By virtue of the authority vested in me by section 301 of Title 3 of the United States Code, it is ordered as follows:

SECTION 1. Executive Order No. 10289 of September 19, 1951, as amended, is hereby further amended (a) By adding at the end of paragraph 1 thereof the following subparagraph (j): "(j) The authority vested in the President by paragraph (b) of section 43 of the Act of May 12, 1933, as amended (31 U.S.C. 821 (b)), to issue silver certificates against any silver bullion, silver, or standard silver dollars in the Treasury not then held for redemption of any outstanding silver certificates, to prescribe the denominations of such silver certificates, and to coin standard silver dollars and subsidiary silver currency for their redemption," and (b) By revoking subparagraphs (b) and (c) of paragraph 2 thereof.

SECTION 2. The amendment made by this Order shall not affect any act done, or any right accruing or accrued or any suit or proceeding had or commenced in any civil or criminal cause prior to the date of this Order but all such liabilities shall continue and may be enforced as if said amendments had not been made.

JOHN F. KENNEDY

THE WHITE HOUSE,

June 4, 1963

As said, Executive Order 11110 is still valid. According to Title 3, United States Code, Section 301 dated January 26, 1998: Executive Order (EO) 10289 dated Sept. 17, 1951, 16 F.R. 9499, was as amended by:

EO 10583, dated December 18, 1954, 19 F.R. 8725;

EO 10882 dated July 18, 1960, 25 F.R. 6869;

EO 11110 dated June 4, 1963, 28 F.R. 5605;

EO 11825 dated December 31, 1974, 40 F.R. 1003;

EO 12608 dated September 9, 1987, 52 F.R. 34617

The 1974 and 1987 amendments, added after Kennedy's 1963 amendment, did not change or alter any part of Kennedy's EO 11110. A search of Clinton's 1998 and 1999 EO's and Presidential Directives has shown no reference to any alterations, suspensions, or changes to EO 11110.

The Federal Reserve Bank, a.k.a Federal Reserve System, is a Private Corporation. Black's Law Dictionary defines the "Federal Reserve System" as: "Network of twelve central banks to which most national banks belong and to which state chartered banks may belong. Membership rules require investment of stock and minimum reserves." privately owned banks own the stock of the FED. This was explained in more detail in the case of Lewis v. United States, Federal Reporter, 2nd Series, Vol. 680, Pages 1239, 1241 (1982), where the court said: "Each Federal Reserve Bank is a separate corporation owned by commercial banks in its region. The stockholding commercial banks elect two-thirds of each Bank's nine member board of directors." In short, Federal Reserve Banks are locally controlled by their member banks.

Also, according to Black's Law Dictionary, these privately owned banks are "allowed" to issue money: "The Federal Reserve Act, created Federal Reserve banks which act as agents in maintaining money reserves, issuing money in the form of bank notes, lending money to banks, and supervising banks as administered by Federal Reserve Board (q.v.)." Thus the privately owned Federal Reserve (FED) banks are allowed to actually issue (create) the "money" we use.

In 1964, the House Committee on Banking and Currency, Subcommittee on Domestic Finance, at the second session of the 88th Congress, put out a study entitled Money Facts which contains a good description of what the FED is: "The Federal Reserve is a total moneymaking machine. It can issue money or checks. And it never has a problem of making its checks good because it can obtain the $5 and $10 bills necessary to cover its check simply by asking the Treasury Department's Bureau of Engraving to print them." Any one person or any closely knit group that has a lot of money has a lot of power. Imagine a group of people with the power to create money. Imagine the power these people would have. This is exactly what the privately owned FED is!

No man did more to expose the power of the FED than Louis T. McFadden, who was the Chairman of the House Banking Committee back in the 1930s. In describing the FED, he remarked in the Congressional Record, House pages 1295 and 1296 on June 10, 1932:

Mr. Chairman, we have in this country one of the most corrupt institutions the world has ever known. I refer to the Federal Reserve Board and the Federal reserve banks. The Federal Reserve Board, a Government Board, has cheated the Government of the United States and he people of the United States out of enough money to pay the national debt. The depredations and the iniquities of the Federal Reserve Board and the Federal reserve banks acting together have cost this country enough money to pay the national debt several times over. This evil institution has impoverished and ruined the people of the United States; has bankrupted itself, and has practically bankrupted our Government. It has done this through the maladministration of that law by which the Federal Reserve Board, and through the corrupt practices of the moneyed vultures who control it.

Some people think the Federal Reserve Banks are United States Government institutions. They are not Government institutions, departments, or agencies. They are private credit monopolies, which prey upon the people of the United States for the benefit of themselves and their foreign customers. Those 12 private credit monopolies were deceitfully placed upon this country by bankers who came here from

Europe and who repaid us for our hospitality by undermining our American institutions.

The FED basically works like this: The government granted its power to create money to the FED banks. They create money, then loan it back to the government charging interest. The government levies income taxes to pay the interest on the debt. On this point, it's interesting to note that the Federal Reserve Act and the sixteenth amendment, which gave congress the power to collect income taxes, were both passed in 1913. The incredible power of the FED over the economy is universally admitted. Some people, especially in the banking and academic communities, support it. On the other hand, there are those like President John F. Kennedy, that have spoken out against it. His efforts were lauded about in Jim Marrs' 1990 book Crossfire:

Another overlooked aspect of Kennedy's attempt to reform American society involves money. Kennedy apparently reasoned that by returning to the constitution, which states that only Congress shall coin and regulate money, the soaring national debt could be reduced by not paying interest to the bankers of the Federal Reserve System, who print paper money then loan it to the government at interest. He moved in this area on June 4, 1963, by signing Executive Order 11110 which called for the issuance of $4,292,893,815 in United States Notes through the U.S. Treasury rather than the traditional Federal Reserve System. That same day, Kennedy signed a bill changing the backing of one and two dollar bills from silver to gold, adding strength to the weakened U.S. currency.

Kennedy's comptroller of the currency, James J. Saxon, had been at odds with the powerful Federal Reserve Board for some time, encouraging broader investment and lending powers for banks that were not part of the Federal Reserve system. Saxon also had decided that non-Reserve banks could underwrite general obligation bonds, again weakening the dominant Federal Reserve banks."

In a speech made to Columbia University on Nov. 12, 1963, ten days before his assassination, President John Fitzgerald Kennedy said: "The high office of the President has been used to foment a plot to destroy the American's freedom and before I leave office, I must inform the citizen of this plight." In this matter, John Fitzgerald Kennedy appears to be the subject of his own book... a true Profile of Courage. According to the Constitution of the United States, (Article 1 Section 8), only Congress has the authority to coin Money, regulate the Value thereof, and of foreign Coin, and fix the Standard of Weights and Measures. However, since 1913 this Article has been ignored by creation and existence of the Federal Reserve Act, which has given a private owned corporation the power and authority to "create" and coin the money of United States. The Federal Reserve is comprised of 12 private credit monopolies who have been given the authority to control the supply of the "Federal Reserve Notes," interest rates and all the other monetary and banking phenomena.

The way the Federal Reserve works is this: 12 private credit monopolies "create", (print), Federal Reserve Notes that are then "lent" to the American government. This is a circular affair in that the government grants the FED power to create the money, which the FED then loans back to the government, charging interests. The government levies income taxes to pay the interest on the debt. It is interesting to note that the Federal Reserve Act and the sixteenth amendment which gave congress the power to collect income taxes, were both passed in 1913. The Federal Reserve Notes are not backed by anything of "intrinsic" value. (i.e., gold or silver).

On June 4, 1963, President, John Fitzgerald Kennedy signed a Presidential decree, Executive Order 11110, which stripped the Federal Reserve Banking System of its power to loan money to the United States Federal Government at interest. This decree meant that for every ounce of silver in the U.S. Treasury's vault, the U.S. government could introduce new money into circulation based on the silver bullion physically held therein. As a result, more than $4 trillion in United States Notes were brought into circulation in $2 and $5 denominations. $10 and $20 United States Notes were never circulated but were being printed by the Treasury Department when Kennedy was assassinated. Kennedy knew that if the silver backed United States Notes were widely circulated, they would have eliminated the demand for Federal Reserve Notes. By giving the U.S. Treasury the Constitutional authority to coin U.S. money once again, EO 11110 would thus prevent the national debt from rising due to "usury" that the American people are charged for "borrowing" (i.e., using) FRN's.

Kennedy knew that, if Congress coined and regulated money, as the Constitution states, the national debt would be reduced by not paying interest to the 12 credit monopolies. This in itself would have allowed the American people freedom to freely use all the money they have earned, enabling the economy to grow. Now, Executive Order 11110 is still in effect, even though no U.S. President has had the courage to follow it. As Americans, it is our duty to question the Federal Reserve System and the power that we have given it by electing presidents that lack the courage of John Fitzgerald Kennedy.

More on JFK's Executive Order 11110:
http://www.rense.com/general44/exec.htm

REPRINTED BY PERMISSION

FOUNDATION FOR TRUTH & LAW 2017